Heroes for Young Readers

Written by Renee Taft Meloche
Illustrated by Bryan Pollard

Adoniram Judson
Amy Carmichael
Betty Greene
Brother Andrew
Cameron Townsend
Corrie ten Boom
C. S. Lewis
David Livingstone
Eric Liddell
George Müller

Gladys Aylward
Hudson Taylor
Jim Elliot
Jonathan Goforth
Loren Cunningham
Lottie Moon
Mary Slessor
Nate Saint
William Carey

Heroes of History for Young Readers

Written by Renee Taft Meloche
Illustrated by Bryan Pollard

Daniel Boone
Clara Barton
George Washington
George Washington Carver
Meriwether Lewis

...and more coming soon

*Heroes for Young Readers Activity Guides and audio CDs
are now available! See the back of this book for more information.*

For a free catalog of books and materials contact
YWAM Publishing, P.O. Box 55787, Seattle, WA 98155
1-800-922-2143   www.ywampublishing.com

HEROES FOR YOUNG READERS

C. S. LEWIS

The Man Who Gave Us Narnia

Written by Renee Taft Meloche
Illustrated by Bryan Pollard

P.O. BOX 55787 / SEATTLE, WA 98155

C. S. Lewis was a boy
    whom everyone called Jack.
He was not good at catching balls
    or swinging baseball bats.

He did not have a normal thumb
    and could not bend it well.
He lived in Ireland, where he
    made stories up to tell.

The year was nineteen hundred five
    and Jack—his brother too—
loved playing in the attic where
    they made up things to do.

The attic ran across their house
    divided by small doors.
There Jack wrote of a whole new world
    that he loved to explore.

In this imaginary world
    lived most unusual things.
He named this kingdom Boxen, where
    a bunny was the king.

Jack's brother went away to school,
    so young Jack soon began
to spend long hours reading books
    of magical new lands.

His happy childhood ended when
    his precious mother died
and he was sent away to school
    where poor Jack often cried.

The man in charge was very cruel
    and he would use a cane
on students for no reason, which
    would cause the children pain.

Jack prayed a lot and read his Bible
    every single day.
He found that this hard time was much
    more bearable that way.

At age sixteen a lifelike image
    popped into Jack's mind.
He saw an upright faun walk through
    the woods in wintertime.

The faun held an umbrella as
    he walked on hooves through snow.
And though he carried parcels, too,
    he never seemed to slow.

The image was so real that Jack
    just knew it would be great
to use it in a story that
    he one day would create.

Two years went by and Jack then left
    to fight the German foe.
The First World War had just begun
    and Jack knew he must go
to France where Germans had attacked.
    He fought far from his home.
When it was quiet, Jack found peace
    through books and writing poems.

But one day Jack was in a place
    where bullets fell like rain.
A huge explosion hit and he
    awakened to great pain.

Rushed to a hospital in England,
    Jack healed slowly there.
He edited and wrote more poems
    in the nurses' care.

When Germany surrendered, he
    no longer had to fight.
His many poems then were published
    much to his delight.

In England Jack attended Oxford
    University.
He soon taught college students English
    and philosophy.

He wrote books that were published about
    Christianity,
and then his country went to war
    again with Germany.

Jack volunteered to make sure homes
    were always dark at night,
with thick black curtains draped 'cross windows
    to help hide the light.

The lights from lampposts and from cars
    could never be turned on,
or German planes could see them and
    would know just where to bomb.

Jack took some London kids to live
    out in his country home
so they could live in safety, far
    from all the fears they'd known.

One of the girls was just so kind
    and helpful Jack felt sure
he'd one day write about a girl
    with qualities like hers.

Jack also started giving speeches
    on the radio.
He shared how Christians ought to live
    and things that they should know.

Jack's talks became so popular
    he traveled more and more
to help encourage soldiers who
    were fighting in the war.

In nineteen forty-five there came
    an end to World War Two.
The Germans had surrendered. Britain's
    darkest days were through!

And then a vision for a fairy
    tale formed in Jack's head—
a story with a faun and with
    a girl kind-spirited.

One day as Jack sat staring at
    a wardrobe large and grand,
he wondered if it too could be
    part of his story plan.

And then each night Jack had a dream.
　　It always was the same—
a dream of a large lion with
　　a big and bushy mane.

Jack named the lion Aslan and
　　he knew it would be part
of one great story he'd thought up
　　and could not wait to start.

He'd write about four children in
　　a land of make-believe,
a place called Narnia, a most
　　enchanted world indeed.

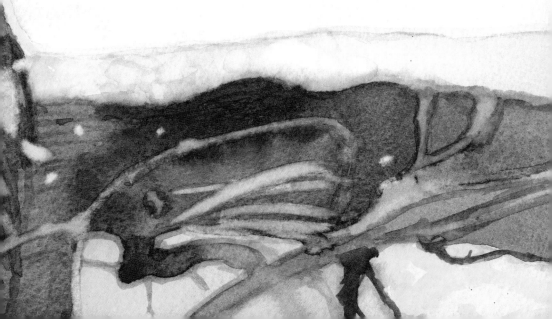

He'd write of noble characters
    and others not so nice.
He'd write of bravery, temptation,
    love, and sacrifice.

He'd write of good and evil and
    which one of them will win.
The Lion, Witch, and Wardrobe is
    the book he would begin.

Now in the book two girls, two boys
    are playing hide-and-seek.
The youngest sister, Lucy, then
    finds something quite unique—
a wardrobe in the attic, just
    a perfect place to hide.
She climbs inside it to the back
    and then begins to slide.

She tumbles down into a strange
    and snowy winter land.
She sees a faun who carries an
    umbrella in his hand.

The faun invites young Lucy over
    for a cup of tea
in Narnia, with talking beavers,
    knights, and nymphs to see.

He tells her of the mean White Witch
    who keeps it winter there
without a Christmas all year long,
    which makes it so unfair.

The Witch turns living things to stone
    and makes all creatures scared.
She does it with her wicked wand
    and with her icy stare.

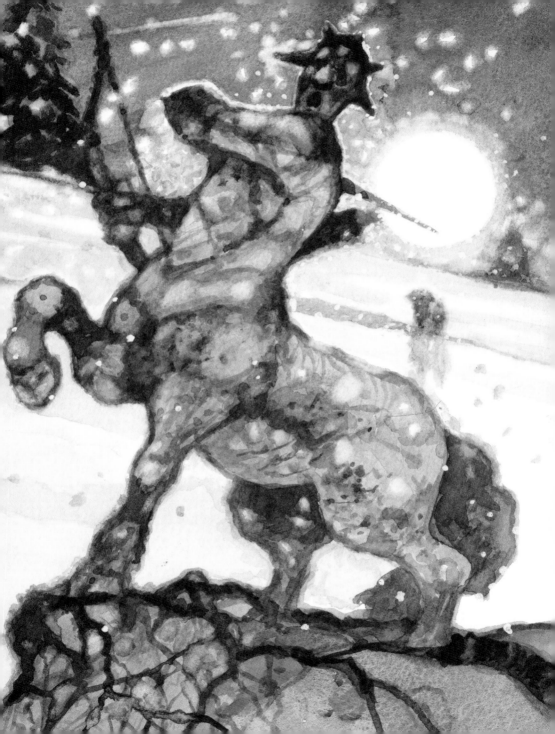

Soon Lucy's siblings follow her
    into this new land too.
They don't know how the wardrobe works
    but all of them go through.

Her brother Edmund meets the Witch
    who's evil and has planned
to kill the lion king called Aslan
    and control the land.

The Witch tempts Edmund with his favorite
    treat, Turkish delight,
so he will tell some secrets that
    will help her win the fight.

There is no end to all the bad
    things that she plans to do.
She plans to turn him and his siblings
    into statues too!

Throughout the story Aslan is
    like Christ—he saves their lives.
This royal King comes back to life
    but first, for them, he dies.

And Lucy and her siblings find
    the will to bravely fight
in service of the living there.
    They choose to do what's right.

They prove themselves in battle and
    are crowned as queens and kings,
the very thing the Witch has tried
    to keep from happening.

The children rule in Narnia
    for many years, and then
they find the secret entrance to
    the wardrobe once again.

They stumble back inside the attic
    where they are surprised
to find outside of Narnia
    that little time's passed by.

This book was just the first of seven
    in a series called
The Chronicles of Narnia—
    great adventures, all.

And every year at Christmastime
    a new book would come out—
a story children and adults
    just loved to read about.

Jack's books reflected his belief
    in Christianity,
and helped teach Christians how to live
    by faith courageously.

In Jack's last book when Lucy asks
    the lion about dying,
he comforts her and then he
    reassures her by replying:
"The life you had in Narnia,
    your great adventures there,
were only the beginning, for
    a new place I've prepared.
There life goes on forever in
    a world that's good and true,
and every chapter there will be
    a better one for you."

One day in nineteen sixty-three
    Jack died at sixty-four.
A Christian, teacher, soldier, he
    would not write anymore.

The storyteller's life on earth
    was through, but thankfully
his great imaginary world
    lives on for you and me.

Like C. S. Lewis, who encouraged
us and entertained
in fiction and nonfiction books,
we too should do the same.

We too should use our talents to
encourage and to bless
our family, friends, and others with
our own creativeness.

Christian Heroes: Then & Now

by Janet and Geoff Benge

Adoniram Judson: Bound for Burma
Amy Carmichael: Rescuer of Precious Gems
Betty Greene: Wings to Serve
Brother Andrew: God's Secret Agent
Cameron Townsend: Good News in Every Language
Clarence Jones: Mr. Radio
Corrie ten Boom: Keeper of the Angels' Den
Count Zinzendorf: Firstfruit
C. S. Lewis: Master Storyteller
C. T. Studd: No Retreat
David Livingstone: Africa's Trailblazer
Eric Liddell: Something Greater Than Gold
Florence Young: Mission Accomplished
George Müller: The Guardian of Bristol's Orphans
Gladys Aylward: The Adventure of a Lifetime
Hudson Taylor: Deep in the Heart of China
Ida Scudder: Healing Bodies, Touching Hearts
Jim Elliot: One Great Purpose
John Wesley: The World His Parish
John Williams: Messenger of Peace
Jonathan Goforth: An Open Door in China
Lillian Trasher: The Greatest Wonder in Egypt
Loren Cunningham: Into All the World
Lottie Moon: Giving Her All for China
Mary Slessor: Forward into Calabar
Nate Saint: On a Wing and a Prayer
Rachel Saint: A Star in the Jungle
Rowland Bingham: Into Africa's Interior
Sundar Singh: Footprints Over the Mountains
Wilfred Grenfell: Fisher of Men
William Booth: Soup, Soap, and Salvation
William Carey: Obliged to Go

Heroes for Young Readers and *Heroes of History for Young Readers* are based on the
Christian Heroes: Then & Now and *Heroes of History* biographies by Janet and Geoff Benge.
Don't miss out on these exciting, true adventures for ages ten and up!

Continued on the next page...

Heroes of History

by Janet and Geoff Benge

Abraham Lincoln: A New Birth of Freedom
Alan Shepard: Higher and Faster
Benjamin Franklin: Live Wire
Christopher Columbus: Across the Ocean Sea
Clara Barton: Courage under Fire
Daniel Boone: Frontiersman
Douglas MacArthur: What Greater Honor
George Washington Carver: From Slave to Scientist
George Washington: True Patriot
Harriet Tubman: Freedombound
John Adams: Independence Forever
John Smith: A Foothold in the New World
Laura Ingalls Wilder: A Storybook Life
Meriwether Lewis: Off the Edge of the Map
Orville Wright: The Flyer
Theodore Roosevelt: An American Original
Thomas Edison: Inspiration and Hard Work
William Penn: Liberty and Justice for All

...and more coming soon. Unit Study Curriculum Guides are also available.

Heroes for Young Readers Activity Guides
Educational and Character-Building Lessons for Children

by Renee Taft Meloche

Heroes for Young Readers Activity Guide for Books 1–4
Gladys Aylward, Eric Liddell, Nate Saint, George Müller

Heroes for Young Readers Activity Guide for Books 5–8
Amy Carmichael, Corrie ten Boom, Mary Slessor, William Carey

Heroes for Young Readers Activity Guide for Books 9–12
Betty Greene, David Livingstone, Adoniram Judson, Hudson Taylor

Heroes for Young Readers Activity Guide for Books 13–16
Jim Elliot, Cameron Townsend, Jonathan Goforth, Lottie Moon

...and more coming soon.

Designed to accompany the vibrant Heroes for Young Readers books, these fun-filled Activity Guides lead young children through a variety of character-building and educational activities. Pick and choose from the activities or follow the included thirteen-week syllabus. An audio CD with book readings, songs, and fun activity tracks is available for each Activity Guide.

For a free catalog of books and materials contact
YWAM Publishing, P.O. Box 55787, Seattle, WA 98155
1-800-922-2143 www.ywampublishing.com